Cambridge Discovery Readers

Level 2

Series editor: Nicholas Tims

T0343091

Ask Alice

Margaret Johnson

CAMBRIDGE
UNIVERSITY PRESS

CAMBRIDGE
UNIVERSITY PRESS & ASSESSMENT

Shaftesbury Road, Cambridge CB2 8EA, United Kingdom

One Liberty Plaza, 20th Floor, New York, NY 10006, USA

477 Williamstown Road, Port Melbourne, VIC 3207, Australia

314–321, 3rd Floor, Plot 3, Splendor Forum, Jasola District Centre, New Delhi – 110025, India

103 Penang Road, #05–06/07, Visioncrest Commercial, Singapore 238467

Cambridge University Press & Assessment is a department of the University of Cambridge.

We share the University's mission to contribute to society through the pursuit of education, learning and research at the highest international levels of excellence.

www.cambridge.org

This American English edition is based on *Ask Alice!*, ISBN 978-84-832-3616-1 first published by Cambridge University Press in 2011.

First published 2011
American English edition 2012
20 19 18 17 16 15 14 13 12 11 10 9 8 7 6 5 4 3

Printed in Great Britain by CPI Group (UK) Ltd, Croydon CRO 4YY

ISBN 978-1-107-68997-8 Paperback American English edition

Cambridge University Press & Assessment has no responsibility for the persistence or accuracy of URLs for external or third-party internet websites referred to in this publication and does not guarantee that any content on such websites is, or will remain, accurate or appropriate.

No character in this work is based on any person living or dead.
Any resemblance to an actual person or situation is purely accidental.

Illustrations by José Rubio

Exercises by Steward Pearson

Cover image by Zoográfico

Music composed by Giannis and published by Shockwave-Sound.com

Contents

People in the story

Alice: a 14-year-old girl; she writes for the student Web site at her school

Lauren: the main writer on the Web site

Ed: the sports writer on the Web site

Johnnie: does all the computer work for the Web site

Yvonne: Alice's mother

James: Alice's father

Emma: a friend of Alice

Stu: one of Ed's friends

Cherie Reeves: a famous pop singer

BEFORE YOU READ

1 Look at the advertisement on page 5. What do you think? Answer the questions.

1 What do people write to Alice about?

....

2 What does Alice do?

....

Chapter 1

Alice knows everything

Do you have a problem?
Do you need someone to help?

She's seen it!
She's done it!
She's felt it!
Alice knows everything!

Send Alice an e-mail. She can help.
askalice@jumpgoldhillhigh.us

"So, what do you think?" Lauren asked me. "Do you like it?"

I looked up from the screen.

Lauren's face was excited. "You want more e-mails, don't you?" she asked me. "We'll put this advertisement on the Web site and lots more people will write to you. What does everyone else think?" She looked at the two boys in the room.

Ed, Johnnie, Lauren, and I all worked on *Jump*, the Web site that gave news and stories to the kids[1] at Gold Hill High School. It was 12:30. We were having our usual Friday lunchtime meeting.

Ed looked bored. Ed's the sports writer for the Web site. Sports is the only thing he's interested in. "It's fine," he told Lauren quickly.

I looked over at Johnnie. Johnnie takes care of the Web site. He knows a lot about computers. "Uh . . . what do you think, Alice?" he asked me in his quiet voice.

"Well," I said, "it looks good, but it's not true. I don't know everything. And I haven't done *everything*."

But Lauren didn't think that was important. "When they make an advertisement for a phone they don't say, 'This phone is OK,'" she argued. "They say, 'This is the best phone in the world!'"

I knew that was true, but phones are different from people. I wanted to say to Lauren, "I'm not a phone!" But she was already talking about something else.

Lauren's like that. She always thinks she's right. She writes most of the stories for the Web site. And she's the editor – the person who decides most things. The Web site was all her idea.

I love writing and that's why I wanted to help with the Web site. But when I talked to Lauren, she said they only needed an advice columnist[2]. An advice columnist – *me*! I'm only 14. Advice columnists in magazines and on Web sites have to answer some difficult questions. They're usually very old.

My friend Emma thought it was funny when I first told her about it. "It's a stupid idea, Alice!" she told me. "It's more work. Don't you have enough homework already? *And* it will be boring! You'll get lots of e-mails from sad people with problems."

But I didn't mind that. I wanted to be a journalist when I finished school, and I thought the Web site was a good way to get some practice. So I went back to Lauren and said yes, and now I'm an advice columnist. I give advice[3] to people with problems. And I like the work most of the time. It's nice to help people.

Here's an e-mail I've just replied to:

▶ **From:** Stay-at-Home Girl
To: askalice@jumpgoldhillhigh.us
Subject: Please help

Hi, Alice,

Can you help me with my problem? My nose is too big and I hate it. All the other kids laugh at me and call me names[4]. I hate school now. I just want to stay in my room all the time. Please help.

Stay-at-Home Girl

This is the reply I put on the Web site:

Hi, Stay-at-Home Girl,

I'm sorry you're so unhappy. I know what it's like when people call you names. I'm biracial race – my mother is black and my father is white – and I get called names sometimes, too.

But what about the kids who laugh at you? Maybe they have something they're not happy about. We all have something that makes us different – too tall, too short, not having the right shoes . . . Maybe laughing at you makes those kids feel happier. I know that's not nice and it's not fair, but sadly people are often like that.

Please, Stay-at-Home Girl, come out of your room and don't worry. My advice is, Tell yourself you've got the best nose in the world!

And if you're still unhappy, please talk to somebody – your mom or dad, or one of the teachers. They can help.

I hope this helps.

Love from,

Alice

As I said, the work of an advice columnist is important. I hate for people to be unhappy, and I like to help them. But I don't know everything, and sometimes I worry. I don't want to say the wrong thing to someone.

"OK, we're almost finished with today's meeting," Lauren was saying. "The last thing we need to talk about is the school dance tomorrow night. Johnnie, are you still OK to take pictures?"

"Yes, that's fine," Johnnie said.

"Great!" said Lauren. "Alice, Ed, look out for any interesting stories."

Ed smiled for the first time in the meeting. "Gossip[5], do you mean?" he asked.

"I prefer to say 'interesting stories,'" Lauren told him. "Who's talking to who, people who look good, people who *don't* look good . . . That kind of thing."

"Gossip," said Ed again.

"Lauren, it isn't very nice to write unkind things about people," I said. "We try to help people with their problems on *Jump*. We don't want them to feel bad."

Both Ed and Johnnie smiled at me. After a moment, Lauren smiled, too. "Don't worry, Alice," she said. "I won't be unkind about anyone."

But I still wasn't happy. I sometimes read gossip magazines at the hair salon. Sometimes gossip was really unkind.

"Will you show us what you write about people – before it goes on the Web site?" I asked.

Lauren looked at me a bit coldly. "Of course, Alice," she said. "That's why we have these Friday meetings, isn't it? OK, does anyone have anything else to say? No? Then let's finish now." And she picked up her bag and left the room.

"Good for you, Alice," Ed said quietly as he left. "It isn't easy to tell Lauren anything."

Johnnie looked at me. "You didn't like the advertisement, did you?" he said.

"No, not really," I agreed. "But I really want people to e-mail me if they need help. So maybe it's OK. Anyway, I'll see you soon, Johnnie."

"See you at the dance," he said.

"But don't take any pictures of *me*, OK?" I said. "I'm not a good dancer! And my friend Emma is helping me choose my clothes. I don't know *what* I'm going to look like!"

"Why don't you just wear what *you* want to wear?" asked Johnnie.

"You don't know what Emma's like," I said. "It's hard to say no to her!"

Johnnie smiled at me. "OK," he said. "No pictures."

As I walked to my next class, I thought about the dance. I didn't really want to go, but Emma wanted us to go together. She loved dances. I didn't have anything good to wear, but Emma wanted to lend me some of her clothes. I couldn't say no. She was so excited.

Why was it so hard for me to say no to people?

"Sometimes, Alice," I told myself as I went into my math class, "I think *you* need to send an e-mail to *Ask Alice!*"

Chapter 2

Dad's idea

The house was empty when I got home from school. I remembered that my mom had a meeting after work. She was a business teacher at a college for older teenagers, and it was always a busy job. Her students had exams that week.

I was getting myself a glass of milk when I got a text message on my phone. It was Emma: *Got some clothes for you to try on. Come over and see them.*

I sat down at the kitchen table to reply to her message: *Sorry, too much homework.*

A text came back: *Boring boring boring!*

I smiled and sent her another message: *OK OK! 7:30.*

Cool! came the reply.

I put my phone down, took an *Ask Alice* e-mail from my bag, and began to read it.

From: PJ
To: askalice@jumpgoldhillhigh.us
Subject: I don't like soccer

Dear Alice,

My father loves soccer, and he really wants me to be good at it. We play soccer every weekend. But I like art, not soccer. I'm good at drawing and painting pictures.

Dad doesn't understand art. He thinks it's boring, and he doesn't like me staying in my room all the time.

I don't want Dad to be angry with me, but I feel very unhappy about this. What can I do?

PJ

14

"Poor PJ," I thought. "His dad doesn't like him as he is."

I looked at the e-mail again and tried to decide what to say to PJ. Then my phone started to ring. I thought Mom was calling to tell me when she was coming home. But it wasn't her.

"Hello?"

"Hi, Alice, it's Dad."

"Dad!" I was really surprised[6].

He laughed and said, "It hasn't been *that* long since I called you, has it?"

"Well," I said, "it has been two or three months."

"Sorry," he said. "I've been away with the band. How are things with you?"

"OK . . . Fine." It was always the same when Dad called. We didn't speak very often, so I was pleased to hear his voice, but I could never think of anything interesting to say. "Mom's not here," I told him quickly. "She's working late."

"She works too hard," he said.

"Yes, Dad," I said, and he laughed again.

"But you've heard me say that before, haven't you?" he said.

I smiled. "Just a few times, Dad."

"Well, listen," he said. "It's you that I want to speak to. I want to hear what you think about my idea."

"What idea?" I asked. I remembered some of Dad's other ideas from the past – like singing lessons. My voice is so bad, people shut their doors and windows when I try to sing!

Dad laughed again. "Don't worry, this is a *good* idea. A vacation."

"A vacation?" I said.

"Yes," he said. "To California. Just you and me."

A vacation! "When?" I asked.

"Next month."

"But Dad, that's before summer vacation."

"Yes, but I'm going to Europe with the band in the summer. They won't mind if you go away for a week, will they? Say yes, Alice!"

I *wanted* to say yes. A vacation in California with Dad! Just the two of us, with lots of time to talk and have fun. He was my dad, but I didn't really know him. He and Mom split up[7] when I was three, and he was always away with his band. A vacation with Dad was a great idea.

The problem was Mom. She was going to say no. I knew it.

"What do you say, Alice?" Dad asked.

"Can I think about it, Dad?" I asked.

"Of course!" he said quickly. "Let me know in a week or two. Anyway, how are things with you? Are you still busy with schoolwork?"

"Yes," I said. "And with *Jump*." I told him about the Web site and my work for *Ask Alice*. We talked for a long time. It was nice.

When it was time for Dad to go, I said, "I'll let you know about the vacation soon, OK?"

"All right, Alice," he said. "Bye for now. I love you."

"I love you, too, Dad," I said.

I was almost crying when I put the phone down. I always felt like that when Dad told me he loved me – happy and sad at the same time. Why was life so difficult? Why didn't I have a dad like all the other dads? A dad who was around all the time. A dad who went to work in the morning and came home in the evening. A dad who understood that I couldn't miss school to go on vacation.

But my dad could never be like that.

I heard Mom's car outside and quickly took some homework out of my bag.

Mom came in with two shopping bags. "Sorry I'm late, Alice," she said. "One of my students needed to talk. Problems with his dad."

I didn't want Mom to start talking about bad fathers, so I smiled at her. "You're an advice columnist, too, aren't you?" I said.

Mom put the bags down and came over to kiss the top of my head. "No, I'm not an advice columnist, I'm a teacher. And teachers often give advice to their students."

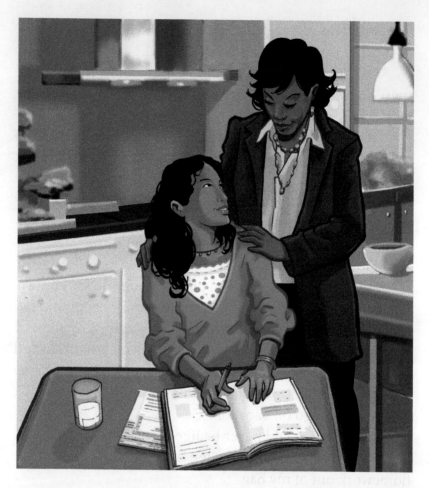

She looked at the *Ask Alice* e-mail. "All this work for the Web site isn't taking too much time, is it? You've got your schoolwork to do. This is an important year for you."

"You said that last year," I told her.

Mom started putting the shopping away. "All school years are important," she said. "If you want to do well in life –"

"– you have to do well in school," I finished for her. "I know. I'm going to do my homework now. OK?"

Mom smiled at me. "OK, Alice."

I smiled back. "And then can I go over to Emma's?" I asked. "She wants me to look at some clothes."

"OK," Mom agreed. "But be back by 9 o'clock."

"OK," I agreed, and took my things up to my room. But as I tried to do my math homework, all I could think about was the vacation. I really wanted to go away with Dad. But how could I make Mom – and the school – say yes?

LOOKING BACK

1 Check your answers to *Before you read* on page 4.

ACTIVITIES

2 Complete the sentences with the names in the box.

> Alice (x2)   ~~Ed~~   Johnnie   Alice's mom
>
> Alice's dad   Lauren   Emma

1 ....*Ed*............ is only interested in sports.
2 .... writes most of the stories for *Jump*.
3 .... wants to be a journalist.
4 .... gives advice to people who have problems.
5 .... is going to take pictures at the dance.
6 .... loves dances.
7 .... is a teacher.
8 .... is in a band.

3 Match the two parts of the sentences.

1 Alice wants Stay-at-Home Girl to   [b]
2 Emma wants Alice to   ☐
3 PJ's dad wants him to   ☐
4 Alice's dad wants her to   ☐

a try on some clothes for the dance.
~~b~~ feel good about her nose.
c go to California during school time.
d play soccer all the time.

4 Are the sentences true (*T*) or false (*F*)?

1 Lauren gave Alice the job of advice columnist on *Jump*. ☒T

2 Ed wants to write a lot of gossip for *Jump*. ☐

3 Alice really wants to go to the school dance. ☐

4 Alice wants Johnnie to take pictures of her. ☐

5 Alice doesn't speak to her dad very often. ☐

6 Alice's dad wants to take her away during summer vacation. ☐

7 Alice is sure her mom will agree to her dad's idea. ☐

8 Alice's mom is worried about Alice spending too much time on *Jump*. ☐

5 Answer the questions.

1 When is the *Jump* meeting each week?

....

2 What is the name of Alice's school?

....

3 What does PJ say he is good at?

....

4 Where is Alice's dad going in the summer?

....

LOOKING FORWARD

6 Check (✓) what you think happens in the next two chapters.

1 Alice goes to the dance. ☐

2 Alice's mom says Alice can go to California with her dad. ☐

3 More people write to *Ask Alice* with problems. ☐

Chapter 3

The dance

"Is that really me?" I thought.

It was Saturday evening and I was looking at myself in the mirror in Emma's bedroom.

Emma was looking, too. "You're so lucky to be tall," she told me. "That skirt looks great on you with your long legs."

"Are you sure?" I asked. It was really short, and I didn't usually wear short skirts. *And* I didn't usually wear so much makeup on my face. The girl in the mirror looked like someone else.

"Stop worrying," Emma said. "You look great. Now, come on, let's get to the dance! We don't want to miss all the fun!"

Emma's dad drove us to school. "See you at 10 o'clock!" he said before he drove away. "Have a good time!"

"We will!" Emma called after him. As we walked to the door of the school gym, our shoes made a "clip-clop" sound. I remembered how Emma and I tried on our moms' clothes when we were young children.

Inside, the music was loud. Lots of people were already there, and some of them were dancing.

"Let's get a drink," Emma said, and I followed her over to where one of the teachers was selling soft drinks. While we were waiting, I looked around for the others from *Jump*. I saw Lauren dancing with a big smile on her face. Johnnie was taking pictures. Ed was with his friends, and they were all laughing about something.

Emma put our two drinks down on a table in a corner and said, "Come on, let's dance! I love this song!"

I didn't really want to dance yet. I just wanted to sit with my drink and watch everybody for a few minutes. But Emma was already on her way to the dance floor, so I followed her.

The other girls on the dance floor smiled at us. Lots of them were wearing short skirts, too. Maybe I did look OK after all.

"Emma's right," I thought. "This is a good song for dancing."

I began to move to the music, and soon I was having
fun. Everyone looked happy, and the lights were turning
their faces different colors. I forgot about everything except
the music.

Emma and I danced to three or four more songs before Ed and some of his friends came over to talk to us.

Ed smiled. "Hi, girls," he said.

Ed's friend Stu was looking at me. *Really* looking at me. He was smiling, but I felt uncomfortable. I wanted to pull my skirt down over my legs, but I couldn't.

"You look good tonight, Alice," Stu said.

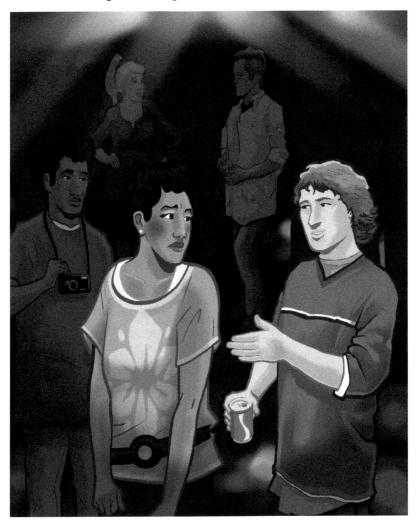

Ed laughed. So did Emma. I felt my face go red.

Johnnie was taking pictures right next to us. As I turned quickly away, I walked into him.

"Alice," he said. "Are you all right?"

"Yes," I said. "I . . . I'm just thirsty. I'm . . . I'm going to sit down."

Emma called after me, "Alice, what's wrong?"

But I didn't stop until I got to our table.

After a few minutes, Emma came to find me. "Are you OK?" she asked.

"Of course," I said. "I was just thirsty."

Emma didn't believe me. "Stu only said you looked good. And he's right. You do."

I didn't answer her. I just drank my drink. Close to our table, two girls were laughing together. They were wearing jeans and nice T-shirts – the kind of clothes I like to wear. I wanted to go home and get changed, but I didn't say anything.

"What's wrong with Stu?" asked Emma. "I think he's good-looking."

I just wanted her to stop talking about it. I didn't like Stu – not in *that* way.

"Don't you want a boyfriend?" Emma was saying now.

"No," I said. "Not really."

"Oh, Alice, you're being boring!" Emma told me. "We came here to have fun!"

I wanted to say to her, "Why don't *you* go and talk to Stu, then?" But I didn't. I said, "You go and dance. I'll come over in a minute."

Emma stood up. "OK," she said. And she walked away.

* * *

26

To: askalice@jumpgoldhillhigh.us
Subject: I don't know what to do

Dear Alice,

I've got a big problem. On the way home from school, my friends and I always go to the shop to get some candy. But last week, they took some candy without paying. The man in the shop didn't see, and my friends all thought it was very funny.

They say they're going to do it again this week, and they want me to do it, too. I don't want to do it. My friends are stealing and it's wrong. But they say I have to steal some candy or they won't be friends with me.

I don't want to lose my friends, but I know stealing is wrong. Can you help?

Yours,

Really Worried

▶ Dear Really Worried,

I know just how you feel. Last week I did something to make a friend happy, but it didn't make me feel happy at all. I think it's really important to be true to yourself. Stealing is wrong and you know it. You could get into big trouble with the police, the school, and your parents. Please don't do it.

Real friends like you just the way you are. A real friend doesn't want you to do things you don't want to do. That's not being a friend. Maybe it's time to make some new friends.

I'll be thinking of you, and I hope you can be strong. I know you can do the right thing.

Love from,

Alice

After I wrote the reply, I sat and thought about my advice to Really Worried. It was true – real friends *did* like you the way you were. And sometimes Emma didn't like me the way I was. Sometimes she wanted me to do things I didn't want to. She was still a friend, but people change. I couldn't just say yes to everything Emma wanted anymore.

Chapter 4

Music and chocolate

"I've got some wonderful news!"

At the next Friday meeting, Lauren was so excited she couldn't sit still. She took a poster out of her bag.

"Come on," said Ed. "Tell us!"

Lauren smiled at us all as she opened up the poster. It was a big picture of Cherie Reeves, the pop singer. "Cherie Reeves is coming to visit the school!"

"Cherie Reeves?" Ed didn't believe it. "Oh, come on, Lauren!" he said. "I know she went to school here, but she's much too famous to want to come back now!"

"She *is* coming," Lauren said. "Next Tuesday. She's going to sing for us! And I'm the person who made it all happen! I heard she was singing in New York next week and I thought, "She won't be far from here." So I made a few phone calls to invite her. And she said yes!"

I was trying to remember something. "Wasn't she unhappy here?" I said. "I think I read something about that in a magazine once."

"I think you're right, Alice," Johnnie said. "I read that, too."

"I'm surprised she wants to come back, then," I said.

"It's because of me," Lauren said. "She just couldn't say no to me!" Ed and Johnnie smiled.

"Nice work, Lauren," said Johnnie.

"Yes, Lauren," said Ed. "You're wonderful. The best editor in the world!"

Lauren smiled. She knew Ed was joking. "All right, all right," she said. "But it is good, isn't it?"

While Lauren talked, I thought about Cherie Reeves. She was the winner of *Big Voices*, a music show on TV, three years ago.

Cherie was 25, and she was biracial like me. She had an unhappy time when she was at our school. So why did she want to come back here? Maybe it was because she had nothing to worry about now. She was famous now, and her unhappy days at Gold Hill High School were all in the past.

"Can I meet her?" I asked Lauren. "Can I meet Cherie when she comes to the school?"

Lauren looked at me. "I'm sure we'll all meet her for a few minutes," she said.

"No," I said. "I mean can I talk to her and ask her some questions? I could write about her time here at school and the problems she had. It could help the people who write to *Ask Alice.*"

Lauren didn't look happy about that. "She won't want to talk about all those things!" she said. "She'll want to talk about her music and all her famous friends. And anyway, I write the stories for *Jump*, don't I?"

Ed and Johnnie both looked at me to see what I was going to say. But Lauren started talking again, about something the principal wanted us to put on the Web site.

After the meeting was over, Johnnie, Ed, and I stayed in the office to use the computers.

Ed looked over at me. "Lauren isn't fair to you sometimes, Alice," he said. "You have some good ideas, but she never wants to listen."

"No, she doesn't, does she?" I agreed, and tried to smile. "But maybe she's right. Cherie Reeves probably wants to forget all about her unhappy time here."

"Most pop singers just want to sell more music," Ed said. "That's why they do things like visiting schools."

"Yes," I agreed. "I'm sure that's why she's coming." I smiled and tried to forget about Lauren. "Anyway," I said, "I have a lot to think about at the moment. I need to think about my problems."

Ed and Johnnie were both working at their computers now, but Ed turned around to look at me.

"You aren't still worrying about the other night with Stupid Stu, are you?"

I felt my face go hot. "No, of course not!" I said. "It's my dad. He wants me to go on vacation with him next month – during school time. But my mom will never agree to it. The thing is, I really want to go. I don't see much of Dad."

"Did I tell you I'm going skiing in Argentina this summer?" Ed asked us.

Johnnie looked over and smiled. "Only about 10 times!" he said. "Or is it 15 times, Alice?"

I laughed. "20, I think, Johnnie!"

We all laughed, and then Johnnie looked at me.

"So," he said. "What are you going to do about the vacation?"

"Well, I have to talk to Mom," I said. "But it's not easy. Every day I think, 'Today. I'll talk to her today.' But I don't. Stupid, isn't it?"

"Just do it," Ed told me. "Do it this weekend. Then you can stop worrying about it."

*   *   *

But I didn't talk to Mom about the vacation over the weekend. I told myself over and over again, "Dad's going to call next week. You have to speak to Mom." But I didn't. I was too afraid she was going to say no.

And I didn't call Emma. The dance was a week ago, but things still weren't quite right between us. I still felt unhappy about that night.

By Monday morning, my head felt heavy with my problems.

At lunchtime, I went to the *Jump* office to see if there were any e-mails for me.

There were, and this was the first one I read.

From: Music Lover
To: askalice@jumpgoldhillhigh.us
Subject: I can't get started

Hi, Alice,

Please help me. I have a big problem with doing things I find difficult, like my homework. I go up to my room to do it, but then I can't get started. I try, but I just start doing something else, like listening to music.

My mom says I need to change. She's right. I do need
to change. I have important exams next year. Can you help?
Music Lover

I read the letter from Music Lover again. I really
understood his problem, because at the moment I had one
just like it. I found it hard to do things that were difficult. I
needed to speak to both Mom and Emma, but I just didn't
do it.

Then I remembered Really Worried's problem from the
week before. That was a bit like mine, too. I had a friend
who tried to make me do things I didn't want to do.

*I had the same problems as the people who were writing
to me for help!*

I sat down in front of the computer and thought about
how to reply to Music Lover. I wanted to give some advice

that I could follow myself. I needed the same kind of help. I needed to speak to Mom, and I needed to speak to Emma.

▶ Dear Music Lover,

Sometimes everyone finds it hard to do things they have to do. I know I do! So let's work on this together.

First, let's think of something we really enjoy – something nice. I choose chocolate because I love chocolate. You could choose music.

Now let's decide when we're going to do the thing that's difficult – for example, by 3 o'clock, or by the end of the week. Then say, "When I've done the difficult thing, I can listen to that music." (Or for me, I can eat some chocolate.)

What do you think? Give it a try. And tell me how it goes.
Love from,
Alice

Twenty-four hours. That's how long I was going to give myself. By tomorrow afternoon, I was going to speak to both Mom and Emma. I was going to speak to them and tell them just how I felt.

And then I was going to eat a *lot* of chocolate!

LOOKING BACK

· ·

1 Check your answers to *Looking forward* on page 21.

ACTIVITIES

· ·

2 Are the sentences true (*T*) or false (*F*)?

1 Alice wears a short skirt to the dance. $\boxed{T}$
2 Alice has a great time at the dance. ☐
3 Ed invites Cherie Reeves to visit Gold Hill High School. ☐
4 Cherie went to Gold Hill High School when she was younger. ☐
5 Alice tells Ed and Johnnie about her dad's vacation idea. ☐
6 Music Lover's problem is a little like Alice's problem. ☐
7 Alice loves chocolate. ☐
8 Alice decides not to talk to her mom about the vacation. ☐

3 Match the two parts of the sentences.

1 Alice feels uncomfortable at the dance because $\boxed{d}$
2 Emma tells Alice that ☐
3 Alice writes to Really Worried about friends, and then ☐
4 Lauren tells Alice that ☐
5 Alice tells Music Lover that ☐

a Cherie won't want to talk about her problems.
b she is being boring.
c she'll eat some chocolate after she does something difficult.
d her skirt is too short and Stu looks at her.
e she starts to think about Emma.

36

4 Put the sentences in order.

1 Emma and Alice get drinks and find a table. ☐
2 Alice and Emma get dressed and put on makeup. ☐1☐
3 Emma comes to find out what's wrong with Alice. ☐
4 Emma's dad drives the girls to the school dance. ☐
5 Stu tells Alice that she looks good. ☐
6 Emma and Alice dance together. ☐
7 Ed and his friends come and talk to Emma and Alice. ☐
8 Alice goes back to the table. ☐

5 Answer the questions.

1 On what day is Cherie Reeves coming to Gold Hill High School?

....

2 Which city is Cherie Reeves singing in next week?

....

3 What TV show did Cherie Reeves win?

....

4 How old is Cherie Reeves?

....

LOOKING FORWARD

6 Check (✓) what you think happens in the next chapter.

1 Cherie Reeves visits the school. ☐
2 Alice meets Cherie Reeves. ☐
3 Alice talks to her mom about the vacation. ☐

Chapter 5

A famous visitor

But my talk with Mom didn't go well.

Perhaps it wasn't a good idea to try to talk to her about the vacation the moment she got home on Monday evening. Mom was always tired after work. But I just had to do it before I changed my mind.

"Mom," I said, as she made a cup of tea, "Dad called me last week."

"Oh, yes?" she said. "And what did he want?"

"Come on, Alice," I told myself. "Just do it!"

The words came out quickly. "He . . . he wants me to go on vacation to California with him next month."

Mom turned to look at me. "Oh, he does?" she said quietly. "Well, I'm sure you said no."

I wasn't going to stop now. "I told him I wanted to think about it," I said.

Mom turned her back on me and finished making her tea.

"There's nothing to think about," she said. "You aren't going."

I never liked it when Mom talked to me like one of her students, but I usually didn't say anything about it. This time it was going to be different.

"That's not fair!" I said. I knew I sounded more like a four-year-old than a 14-year-old, but it *wasn't* fair. I didn't see Dad very often, and now he wanted to spend some time with me.

Mom brought her tea over to the table. She had her answer ready. "Life isn't fair, Alice. I know that, believe me."

I knew what she meant, and I felt angry. I stood up and shouted, "You never forget, do you? You and Dad split up over 10 years ago. This isn't about me – it's about you and Dad!"

Mom didn't get angry. "No, it's not about your father and me, Alice," she said. "It's about you not going away during school time just because he wants a vacation. The school won't allow it."

"He doesn't just want a vacation!" I said. "He wants a vacation with *me*! And how do you know the school won't allow it? We haven't asked! Perhaps they'll understand that I don't see Dad very often. Please, Mom!"

She sat down opposite me. "Alice, I know you don't see him very often," she said. "And I hate that. I hate the way he comes in and out of your life. I hate it when you don't hear from him for weeks and weeks. I know how it hurts you."

I couldn't look at her – I was too close to crying.

"But I'm your mother, Alice," she went on. "I have to do what I think is best for you. I'm not going to let your father take you on vacation during school time. I'm sorry."

I turned and ran out of the room. Mom called after me, but I didn't stop.

* * *

Next morning I came down to breakfast late. Mom was in the kitchen, but I didn't want to talk to her.

"Alice," she said. "Don't be like this."

I just took some fruit and went to the door. "I'm late," I said, and then I left.

As I walked, I felt sick and empty inside, but it wasn't because of not eating breakfast. It was because I felt so sad. I didn't really know Dad. Sometimes Mom didn't want me to know him. And sometimes, when Dad was away for a really long time, I felt that he didn't want to know me . . .

I tried to think about something else. Today was a special day. Cherie Reeves was coming to school. I had to think about that and forget about everything else. It was going to be fun.

At school, everyone was in the gym. They were waiting for Cherie Reeves to arrive.

"Cherie!" they were shouting. "We want Cherie!"

At the front, near the stage, Lauren was talking to someone from the television news. She couldn't stop smiling,

and I smiled, too. Lauren was right. She was smart to bring
Cherie to our school. Cherie was *really* famous.

And then there she was – Cherie Reeves walked onto
the stage. She was small, and she was wearing jeans and a
T-shirt. She looked like a normal person really, not a star[8].

"Hello, Gold Hill High School!" she shouted. Then she
began to sing. And it was amazing[9]. Everyone got up on
their feet and began to dance. Cherie had the most beautiful
voice. I remembered the night when I watched her win *Big
Voices*. And now she was singing on the stage in front of me.
She *was* a star. A big star.

At the end of the song, we all clapped[10] and shouted for more, and Cherie smiled. Then she put one hand up and waited until we were quiet.

"Thank you!" she said. "Thank you so much. It's great to be back here, and I've got one thing I want to say to you all today. If you really want something, you have to try hard. Then try harder. Don't ever let people forget you're there. Tell them, 'I can do it!' Tell them, 'What about me?' Say it over and over again until people remember you. That's what I did!"

Then Cherie began to sing "Always My Friend," a quiet song about being hurt when love dies. Emma and I loved that song. We sang it together sometimes. It always made us cry! I had to look over at her, and when I did, she was looking at me.

We smiled, and I knew then that everything was going to be OK. Emma was my friend. I needed to say no to her sometimes, but she was still my friend.

Cherie sang three more songs before she finished. The principal went up on stage to thank her, and then Cherie waved to us one last time and left the stage.

As we were all leaving the gym, Emma came up to me. "Wasn't she great?" she said.

"Really great," I said. "I loved our song."

She smiled at me. "See you later?" she asked.

I smiled back. "Yes. See you later."

I was almost at the classroom when Lauren ran up to me. She wasn't smiling now – she looked really worried. "Alice!" she said quietly into my ear. "Have you seen Cherie?"

"What do you mean?" I asked. "We all just saw her on the stage."

"Yes, but have you seen her since then?"

"No," I answered. "I haven't seen her."

"Then help me look for her!" Lauren told me. "She's disappeared!"

"Disappeared?"

"Nobody knows where she is, and the TV people are waiting to speak to her!"

"But I'll be late for class," I said.

"I'll be late, too, but this is more important!" Lauren said, and then she ran off.

A voice in my head told me, "You don't have to do what Lauren tells you!"

But I wanted to know where Cherie was. It was strange for her to just disappear. Was something wrong?

I tried the library, but Cherie wasn't there. And she wasn't in the cafeteria. Or the restrooms. Then I tried the girls' locker room[11].

And there she was. She was sitting by the window.

I sat down beside her and said, "Hi, I'm Alice. Are you . . . OK?"

She didn't smile as she looked at me.

"Are they all looking for me?" she asked.

"Yes," I agreed. "But they don't know you're here."

She smiled then, quickly. "That Lauren girl wants to ask me lots of questions," she said. "And the TV people. I'll talk to them in a moment, but I just wanted to come in here and . . . think for a while."

She sounded sad, and I knew that this was the real Cherie – a quiet girl with a sad face, not a big star. She was like somebody who e-mailed *Ask Alice*. I think that's why I asked my next question.

"Did . . . something bad happen to you in here?"

Cherie's dark eyes looked into mine.

"You don't have to answer that," I told her quickly.

But she said, "No, it's OK. When I was at school, this . . . was the room I came to when things got bad."

She stopped and was quiet for a moment. Then she picked up her bag and got up. But I spoke quickly before she could go. "Did someone bully[12] you, Cherie?"

Cherie sat down again. She looked at me. It was raining outside. I could hear it falling against the window. There was no one else around – just Cherie and me.

When she answered my question, her voice was quiet.

"Yes," she agreed. "Some kids bullied me. They . . . waited for me every day after school. So sometimes I came in here. I stayed here until I thought it was safe to go."

I saw her in my head, a small girl listening and waiting in the locker room, always afraid.

"And was it safe?" I asked. "When you came out of here?"

"Sometimes," she said. "Not always."

Not always.

It was hard to know what to say to her. But I felt she wanted to talk some more.

"I don't know why kids are like that," I said.

"They don't like people to be different," Cherie said. "And I was different. I'm biracial, we were poor, Mom was ill, I was good at singing . . . Any of those things are enough for a bully, aren't they?"

"Yes," I agreed sadly. "They are."

She looked at me. "And now you'll probably tell everyone about this, won't you?" Her voice was a bit angry now.

"I'm not going to do that, Cherie," I told her. "I know how gossip can hurt people. I'm the advice columnist for our student Web site."

Cherie smiled. "What?" she said. "So, I've just told all my problems to an advice columnist? That's lucky!" And we both laughed.

"It's good to know that the kids here can ask someone for help now," Cherie said. "I had nobody."

"The school does a lot to stop bullying these days," I told her.

"I'm very happy to hear it," Cherie said. Her voice was stronger now. "When I was sad, my music really helped me, you know?" she told me. "When I sang I thought, 'I'll show you. One day I'll be a really good singer. I'll be famous and I'll show you!'"

I smiled. "And you *are* really good. Cherie, you were amazing today."

She smiled back. "Thanks. And thanks for listening, too," she said. "You know, Alice, I'm happy for you to write about our talk in here for your Web site."

"Really?" I said.

"Really," she replied. "Perhaps reading about my problems will help someone."

She kissed my cheek, stood up, and then, seconds later, she was gone.

LOOKING BACK

1 Check your answers to *Looking forward* on page 37.

ACTIVITIES

2 Are the sentences true (*T*) or false (*F*)?

1 Alice's mom wants Alice to go away with her dad. ☐F☐
2 Alice agrees with her mom about the vacation. ☐
3 Alice thinks Cherie sings very well. ☐
4 Emma enjoys Cherie's concert. ☐
5 Lauren can't find Cherie after the concert. ☐
6 Alice can't find Cherie after the concert. ☐
7 Cherie tells Alice about the problems she had at school. ☐
8 Cherie feels better after she speaks to Alice. ☐

3 Complete the sentences with the names in the box.

> Alice (x2)   ~~Alice's mom~~   Emma
> Lauren (x2)   Cherie (x2)

1 *Alice's mom* says that life isn't fair.
2 .... doesn't eat breakfast on Tuesday morning.
3 .... talks to a person from the TV news.
4 .... doesn't look like a star, but she sings like one.
5 .... smiles at Alice while Cherie is singing.
6 .... tells Alice to look for Cherie.
7 .... is from a poor family.
8 .... tells Cherie that gossip can hurt people.

4 Match the two parts of the sentences.

1 Alice's mom feels angry when ☐ d

2 The students all clap and shout after ☐

3 Cherie tells Alice that ☐

4 Alice tells Cherie that ☐

a Cherie sings her first song.

b some kids bullied her at school.

c the school tries to stop bullying now.

d Alice's dad doesn't call for a long time.

5 Answer the questions.

1 When does Alice talk to her mom about the vacation?

....

2 What is the name of the song Alice and Emma both love?

....

3 Where do Alice and Cherie talk?

....

4 What does Cherie say that Alice can do?

....

LOOKING FORWARD

6 Check (✓) what you think happens in the next chapter.

1 Alice writes about her talk with Cherie. ☐

2 Alice's mom agrees to Alice's vacation with Dad. ☐

3 Alice stops being the advice columnist on *Jump*. ☐

Chapter 6

Helping the helper

Hi, Dad. I'm coming into town after school. Can you meet me in the bookstore café to talk about the vacation in California? Will be there at 4. See you then.

I sent the message to Dad, and then I wrote another one: *Hi, Mom. I have to get a book tonight for homework. I need some help! Meet me at the bookstore at 4.*

Mom finishes work early on Tuesdays. She often helps me with homework. "She'll come," I thought.

And sure enough, my phone soon made a noise to tell me I had a message: *Of course. See you in the bookstore. Mom.*

I quickly sent a message back: *Let's meet in the café first.*

My phone made another noise. This time the message was from Dad: *4 in the bookstore café is good for me. See you then. Dad.*

I smiled. Great. They were both coming.

Now I just had to get them to stay in the same room together and talk.

When I got to the café, Mom was already there. "Hi," she said.

"Sorry about last night, Mom," I said.

She smiled. "Let's not talk about it," she said. "What do you want to drink? A hot chocolate?"

"Yes, please," I said.

"OK," she said. "One hot chocolate coming up."

I sat at a table near the door.

"Please don't be late, Dad," I thought. "Please don't be late."

He wasn't. "Hi, Alice," he said with a big smile.

But he didn't stay smiling for long because Mom came back with our drinks.

She didn't look happy. "What are you doing here?" she asked Dad.

"What are *you* doing here?" Dad asked her.

"Alice wanted to meet me here," said Mom.

"That's strange," he said. "She wanted to meet me here, too."

They both looked at me. "Alice?" Mom said.

"I invited you both," I told them. "So we can talk. About the vacation. Mom, please sit down."

But she didn't sit down. "I've already told you, Alice, there's nothing to talk about!"

"Oh, yes, that's just like you, Yvonne," said Dad. "You always say no to things without thinking about them. I just want to –"

"I'm not interested in what you want!"

Now they were arguing.

"Stop it!" I said loudly. Too loudly. The women who worked in the café looked over at us.

Mom and Dad were surprised, too. They both stopped and were quiet.

"Please," I said. "Can you both just listen to me?" I wasn't speaking so loudly now, but my voice was still strong.

Mom put the drinks down on the table and sat down. "All right," she said. "I'm listening."

"Me, too," said Dad.

I looked at them both, and then I looked at Mom. "Mom, you're right – I can't go on vacation during school time." I looked at Dad. "Dad, you were wrong to ask me to do it. Mom's right – school is important."

Mom smiled. Dad sat down. "I'm sorry," he said. "A friend of mine has a house in California. He said we can use it next month, that's all. I didn't think."

"You never think!" Mom said.

I spoke quickly, before they started arguing again. "But I do want to go on vacation with you, Dad."

He looked up and smiled. "You do?" he asked.

"Yes," I said. "It just has to be during the school break. Mom, I want to spend some time with Dad. He's my *dad*. I need to know him."

I looked at Dad and tried very hard not to start crying. "And Dad, you . . . need to make sure we see each other more often. I know you have to travel for your work, but . . . I need to know when I'm going to see you again. Sometimes . . . sometimes you're gone for so long . . ."

Dad's face was sad. "I'm sorry, Alice," he said. "I'll try. I'll really try."

Mom looked at him across the table. "It's not enough just to try, James," she told him. "You have to make sure it happens."

54

They sat and looked at each other. Dad's face was still sad. "I can't change the past, Yvonne," he said. "All I can do is try to be different now. Alice is a wonderful girl. You've done a great job with her. Now I want to do my part."

Mom looked at him for a long time before she spoke. I knew what she was thinking, "Can I believe him? Does he really want this? Or is my daughter going to get hurt all over again?"

I put my hand on her arm and said, "Please, Mom."

"All right," she said to Dad. "You can take Alice on vacation. During the school break."

Dad started to smile. "November OK?" he asked.

"Yes," Mom agreed. "November's OK. During the break."

"Yes!" I shouted loudly. The women from the café looked over at us again, and Mom, Dad, and I all laughed.

*   *   *

I was still feeling good on Friday before the *Jump* meeting. There was just enough time to answer an e-mail before it began, and I started to read one.

▶ **From:** Unhappy Goalkeeper
To: askalice@ jumpgoldhillhigh.us
Subject: I want to do more

Dear Alice,

I love soccer, but Mr. Phelps usually makes me the goalkeeper. Being the goalkeeper is OK, but I want to be the one who gets goals[13]! I love to run and try to get the ball. It's exciting! I don't want to just wait for the ball to come to me.

I tried talking to Mr. Phelps, but he won't listen to me. He just says I have to be the goalkeeper. What can I do?
Unhappy Goalkeeper

I sat and looked at the letter. Now somebody else had a problem like mine. I knew just how Unhappy Goalkeeper was feeling. Lauren never listened to me or let me write what I wanted to write.

Just then Lauren came into the room. "Let's start the meeting," she said. "Alice? Are you coming?"

I looked up and saw that she was waiting for me. "Oh, sorry, Lauren," I said.

We all moved to sit around the table. Lauren began. "Now, this week I want –"

"Lauren," I said. "Can I just say something first?"

Lauren didn't look happy. "Well?" she said. "What is it?"

Ed and Johnnie both looked at me.

I didn't feel afraid of Lauren. As I took some pieces of paper from my bag, I felt strong. "I know you write the big stories, Lauren," I said, "but when Cherie was here, I spoke to her. She said I could write a story about her."

I held my story out to Lauren.

She didn't take it.

"You spoke to Cherie?" she asked.

"Yes," I said. "When everyone was looking for her, I found her in the girls' locker room. We talked. She told me all about the problems she had when she was here at school. She said it was OK for me to write about them. So I have."

Ed took the story from me and looked at it quickly. "This is a really big story!" he said. "You have to put it on the Web site, Lauren!"

Lauren looked angry with me. I didn't want that.

"Look, Lauren," I told her, "I'm not trying to steal your job. I just got lucky, that's all. But I do really want to write more for the Web site. I don't just want to reply to e-mails. I want to write longer things about the problems people have – with friends, with families – things like that. You can do everything else. What do you think?"

Lauren didn't say anything. But Ed and Johnnie did.

"It's a great idea," said Ed.

"I agree," said Johnnie. "People will really like that kind of thing."

We all looked at Lauren. At last she spoke. "OK," she said. "I'll think about it, all right? Now, can we start the meeting?"

*   *   *

As I walked to my class after the meeting, I felt good. I was thinking about stories I could write. Then I heard someone behind me. It was Johnnie.

"Hi," I said. "Thanks for saying you liked my idea."

He smiled. "It's a great idea. *You* were great, talking to Lauren like that." Then he looked uncomfortable. "Actually," he said, "I have something to tell you. It's about those e-mails . . ."

59

"Which e-mails?" I asked.

"The ones from Really Worried, Music Lover, and Unhappy Goalkeeper."

I looked at him. And then I knew. "It was you!" I said. "*You* wrote them, didn't you?"

Johnnie's face was red. "Yes," he said. "Sorry."

"But why?" I asked.

"You had lots of problems," he said. "I just wanted to help, that's all. You wanted to say no when you didn't want to do something. You knew you had to talk to your mom, but you couldn't do it. You wanted to write more for the Web site. So I . . . I wrote e-mails to you from people with the same sort of problems. You . . . don't mind, do you?"

I thought about those three e-mails from Really Worried, Music Lover, and Unhappy Goalkeeper – about reading them and answering them, and how that helped me so much.

And all the time they were from Johnnie! I thought I was helping other people, but really Johnnie was helping me!

"Was that OK, Alice?" he asked.

"Yes, Johnnie," I said. "It was more than OK. Thank you for being a good friend." I smiled at him. "Actually, you're a better advice columnist than me. Do you want my job?"

Johnnie smiled, too. "No, thank you!" he said. Then he took something from his backpack and gave it to me. "You've done a lot in the last few days," he said. "I think you've earned this."

It was a bar of chocolate.

I took the chocolate and said, "I certainly have!"

And we both laughed.

LOOKING BACK

1 Check your answers to *Looking forward* on page 49.

ACTIVITIES

2 Are the sentences true (*T*) or false (*F*)?

1   Alice sends text messages to her mom and to her dad. ☐T

2   Alice's dad arrives late to meet Alice. ☐

3   Alice's mom is happy to see Alice's dad. ☐

4   Alice tells her parents to listen to her. ☐

5   Alice's dad agrees to try to see Alice more often. ☐

6   Alice's mom agrees to let Alice go away with her dad. ☐

7   Lauren is happy to get Alice's story about Cherie. ☐

8   Ed says Alice's story has to go on the Web site. ☐

9   One person wrote three e-mails to *Ask Alice*. ☐

10   Alice is surprised to find out who has written to her. ☐

3 Match the two parts of the sentences.

1   Alice meets her mom and dad ☐d

2   Alice's dad can take Alice on vacation ☐

3   Alice reads the e-mail from Unhappy Goalkeeper ☐

4   Johnnie comes and talks to Alice ☐

a   before the *Jump* meeting.

b   after the *Jump* meeting.

c   in November.

~~d~~   at 4 o'clock in the afternoon.

4 <u>Underline</u> the correct words in each sentence.

1 Alice tells her mom she needs help with her *homework* / *writing for the Web site*.

2 The women in the café look at Alice because she is *crying* / *speaking too loudly*.

3 Unhappy Goalkeeper wants to *get goals* / *stop playing soccer*.

4 Alice tells Lauren she wants to *stop writing* / *write more* for *Jump*.

5 Really Worried, Music Lover, and Unhappy Goalkeeper all have problems that are *different from* / *like* Alice's problems.

6 Alice tells Johnnie he has been a *good* / *bad* friend.

5 Answer the questions.

1 Where does Alice meet her mom and dad?

....

2 What does Alice's mom buy Alice to drink?

....

3 Who wrote the e-mails from Really Worried, Music Lover, and Unhappy Goalkeeper?

....

4 What does Johnnie give to Alice at the end of the story?

....

Glossary

[1]**kid** (page 6) *noun*   a child or young person

[2]**advice columnist** (page 7) *noun*   someone who gives **advice** on people's problems in a magazine or on a Web site

[3]**advice** (page 7) *noun*   words that help someone decide what to do

[4]**call names** (page 8) *verb*   to use unkind words to describe someone

[5]**gossip** (page 10) *noun*   talk about other people's lives that can be untrue

[6]**surprised** (page 15) *adjective*   having the feeling that comes when something new or unusual happens

[7]**split up** (page 16) *verb*   to stop being together as, for example, husband and wife or boyfriend and girlfriend

[8]**star** (page 41) *noun*   a famous singer, actor, sports person, etc.

[9]**amazing** (page 41) *adjective*   very good

[10]**clap** (page 42) *verb*   to put your hands together to show that you enjoyed something

[11]**locker room** (page 44) *noun*   a room where you change into sports clothes

[12]**bully** (page 45) *verb*   to say and do things to make a weaker person feel afraid

[13]**goal** (page 56) *noun*   a point you get in sports like soccer